A MERRY CHRISTMAS COOKBOOK

Recipes by Cristina Garces
Photography by Teri Lyn Fisher
Illustrations by the Disney Storybook Artists

DISNEY PRESS

New York • Los Angeles

BEFORE YOU BEGIN . . .

'Tis the season for sledding, ice-skating, gift wrapping, and especially cooking fun Christmas recipes! This book is full of scrumptious winter goodies from all your favorite Disney characters, and they're sure to warm you up after a day in the snow, or spice up a day spent indoors.

With more than twenty-five recipes, you'll have plenty of homemade holiday treats to share with the ones you love. Plus, they make perfect gifts! Included in this book is a handful of dishes whose ingredients can also be assembled in jars and be given as gifts with punch-out tags found in the back of the book! You can tell by the at the end of the recipes.

Don't worry if your cooking skills are barely there. All you need is some Christmas spirit! Every recipe is rated on a five-gingerbread-man scale: . That way you can start by making something easy ( ) and work your way up to the more complicated concoctions ( ).

Here are a few things to remember:
- You'd better watch out and make sure not to touch a hot stove!
- Always ask a grown-up for help when using mixers, blenders, stoves, ovens, and knives.
- Wash your hands before you start, and clean up when you're done. Santa knows when you don't! Plus, cleanliness is extremely important. So be clean for cleanness's sake!
- Put on an apron, roll up your sleeves, and pull back your hair.
- Gather all your ingredients and read a recipe all the way through once before you start.
- Last, you'd better not pout, and remember to have some fun!

So put on your oven mitts and Santa hat, and warm up the kitchen with some wonderful Christmas dishes!

CONTENTS

BREAKFAST

SLEEPY'S EARLY-RISER EGG BISCUITS

🍪🍪🍪 Makes 10

There's one time a year that Sleepy is an early riser—Christmas morning! These mini egg biscuits made with cheese and turkey bacon are the perfect size for little hands.

INGREDIENTS

1 tube refrigerated biscuits

4 large eggs

2 teaspoons whole milk

¼ teaspoon salt

¼ teaspoon black pepper

¼ cup cooked broccoli florets, chopped

6 strips cooked turkey bacon, crumbled

¼ cup shredded cheddar cheese

DIRECTIONS

1. Preheat the oven to 350°F. Grease the cups of a standard-sized muffin tin. Separate the biscuit dough, and place each of the 10 biscuits into the muffin openings. (You'll have two empty cups left over.)

2. Bake the biscuit crusts for 5 minutes. While the biscuits are cooking, crack the eggs into a mixing bowl and add the milk, salt, and pepper. Whisk to combine, and stir in the broccoli and half of the cheddar cheese.

3. Remove the biscuits from the oven and use a wooden spoon to create a hole for the egg mixture.

4. Pour the egg mixture into each biscuit crust and top evenly with crumbled turkey bacon and the remaining cheddar cheese. Bake for 12–15 minutes. Once you have an adult help take them out, make sure to let the biscuits cool for a few minutes before enjoying.

BELLE'S CLASSIC WINTER PORRIDGE

 Serves 4 – 6

One of Belle's favorite breakfasts is a warm, spiced porridge with brown sugar and dried fruits. She even picks the berries herself!

INGREDIENTS

4 cups milk

2 cups old-fashioned oats

1½ cups dried fruit mix (like raisins, cranberries, and apricots)

1½ teaspoons cinnamon

½ teaspoon ground ginger

¼ teaspoon ground nutmeg

¼ teaspoon ground cloves or allspice

1½ teaspoons vanilla extract

¼ cup brown sugar

2 cups water

Chopped nuts, for topping

DIRECTIONS

1. With an adult's help, warm the milk over medium heat in a large saucepan. Stir in the oats and cook for about 5 minutes, stirring constantly.

2. Stir in the fruit, spices, vanilla extract, brown sugar, and water. Turn the heat down to medium-low and simmer for 5 more minutes.

3. Portion out into four to six individual bowls. Top with additional dried fruit and chopped nuts.

TIP: You can add a tablespoon of your favorite jam or even a splash of Stitch's Hawaiian Eggnog (page 48) for different flavors!

MONSTER-O'S SPICED BREAKFAST BARS

Makes 8 bars

Mike and Sulley know there's no faster way to Boo's heart than a big helping of Monster-O's. These stocking stuffer–sized breakfast bars filled with whole-grain-oat cereal, honey, cinnamon, and nuts are her special Christmas treat.

INGREDIENTS

¼ cup dark brown sugar

¼ cup unsalted butter

½ cup honey

2 teaspoons vanilla extract

¼ teaspoon salt

¼ cup peanut or almond butter

2 cups whole-grain-oat cereal

¾ cup almonds, chopped

½ teaspoon cinnamon

DIRECTIONS

1. Preheat oven to 350°F. Grease 9- by 13-inch baking pan, or line it with parchment paper.

2. Have an adult help you combine the dark brown sugar, butter, honey, vanilla extract, and salt in a medium-sized saucepan over medium heat. Cook, stirring occasionally, until butter melts and the sugar completely dissolves. Stir in the peanut or almond butter.

3. Add the cereal, almonds, and cinnamon to the pot and stir to combine. Remove the pot from the heat with an adult's help, and pour the mixture onto the baking sheet, distributing it evenly along the bottom. Press down firmly.

4. Have an adult help you place the baking pan into the oven, and bake for 5–7 minutes. Let the mixture cool to room temperature before cutting into bars. These will keep for about a week at room temperature or a couple of weeks in the fridge or freezer.

TIP: It's easy to add any of your favorite ingredients to these bars. Mike and Sulley like nuts; dried fruit such as raisins, apricots, and coconut; or even chocolate chips! Have fun trying new combinations.

ROLLY'S SPOTTED CRANBERRY PANCAKES

🍪🍪🍪 Serves 4 – 6

Little Rolly is always hungry, and these pancakes loaded with dried cranberries, walnuts, and chocolate chip "spots" are healthy and filling enough to last him until Christmas dinner!

INGREDIENTS

1 cup all-purpose flour

2 tablespoons sugar

2 teaspoons baking powder

¼ teaspoon salt

½ teaspoon ground cinnamon

1 cup milk

2 teaspoons vanilla extract

2 tablespoons unsalted butter, melted

1 large egg

½ cup walnuts, chopped

½ cup dried cranberries

¾ cup mini or regular chocolate chips

DIRECTIONS

1. In a small bowl, whisk together the flour, sugar, baking powder, salt, and cinnamon.

2. In a medium bowl, mix together the milk, vanilla extract, butter, and egg. Whisk in the flour mixture until just wet, and carefully stir in the walnuts, cranberries, and chocolate chips.

3. Have an adult help you heat a large skillet over medium-low heat and grease with cooking spray. Spoon 2 tablespoons of batter into the skillet for each pancake, using the back of the spoon to spread the batter into a circular shape.

4. Cook each pancake until golden brown, about 1 minute per side. Serve with maple syrup or powdered sugar.

ASSEMBLING A GIFT JAR:

Layer the following ingredients from above in a pint-sized (16-ounce) mason jar in this order: flour, baking powder, sugar, salt, cinnamon, chocolate chips, cranberries, walnuts. Close the jar tightly, and attach the recipe card from the back of the book.

LUNCH

CAJUN SWEET DOUGH TURNOVERS

🍪🍪🍪🍪 Makes 4

This classic Cajun winter treat is Tiana and Charlotte's favorite dish to cook together for Christmas. You can enjoy it with the more traditional sweet potato filling, or use vegetables or even sliced cold cuts to create your own custom turnovers.

INGREDIENTS

For Cajun sweet dough:

1 cup plus 2 tablespoons all-purpose flour

½ teaspoon baking powder

¼ teaspoon salt

3 tablespoons unsalted butter, softened

1 tablespoon sugar

¼ teaspoon vanilla extract

1 tablespoon beaten egg

2 tablespoons whole milk

For sweet potato filling:

1 15-ounce can yams in syrup, drained and mashed

¼ teaspoon cinnamon

¼ teaspoon nutmeg

¼ teaspoon ginger

For broccoli and cheese filling:

1 cup broccoli, cooked

½ cup cheddar cheese, shredded

1 cup cooked chicken or ham, cubed (optional)

DIRECTIONS

1. In a small bowl, whisk together the flour, baking powder, and salt, and set aside.

2. Using a handheld mixer, cream together the butter and sugar until the mixture is light and fluffy, about 3 minutes. Add the vanilla and the egg and mix to combine. Alternate mixing in a little of the flour mixture with a little of the milk until both are combined. Transfer the dough to a sheet of plastic wrap, roll it up, and place it in the refrigerator for 15 minutes.

3. Preheat the oven to 375°F. Combine the ingredients for your preferred filling in a small bowl. Remove the dough from the refrigerator and separate into 4 pieces. Roll the dough out into 4 circles with a rolling pin on a floured surface. You can use the mouth of a small bowl to cut out perfect circles, or leave them as they are for a more homemade look.

4. Using a spoon, scoop a fourth of the filling into the center of each small circle. Add water to the edges of the dough, fold the circle in half, and crimp the edges together with a fork.

5. Place on a baking sheet, and bake for 12–15 minutes or until golden brown on the outside. Once turnovers are done, make sure to let them cool down before taking a bite!

ELSA'S SNOWY MAC & CHEESE

Serves 6

After ice skating with Anna and Olaf, Elsa loves to make the perfect lunch to share with her friends—mac & cheese!

INGREDIENTS

1 tablespoon olive oil

2 tablespoons butter, melted

3 tablespoons flour

1½ cups milk

2 cups white cheddar cheese, shredded

1 cup mozzarella cheese, shredded

¼ teaspoon ground nutmeg

¼ teaspoon ground cayenne pepper

1¾ teaspoons salt

3 cups elbow macaroni (plain or whole wheat)

2 cups cauliflower, cooked and chopped

DIRECTIONS

1. Cook the macaroni according to the directions on the box.

2. With an adult's help, add the oil, butter, and flour to a large pot over medium-low heat, and whisk together for 3 minutes. While continuing to whisk, slowly add in the milk and gently bring to a bubble. Stir in the cheddar and mozzarella cheeses one handful at a time. Season with nutmeg, cayenne pepper, and salt.

3. Add the cooked pasta and cauliflower to the pot and stir to coat with the cheese sauce.

TIP: If you'd like a crispy top, pour the entire mixture into a baking dish, cover with an additional 1 cup of mozzarella cheese, and have an adult help you place it in the broiler until it has browned, for about 3 minutes.

TIANA'S GREEN BEAN CASSEROLE

 Serves 6

There's nothing Tiana loves more than to cook for her family during the holidays, and this classic southern vegetable dish is a childhood favorite she shared with her dad.

INGREDIENTS

2 cups green beans, sliced and cooked

1 10½-ounce can cream of mushroom soup

¼ cup milk

½ teaspoon salt

½ teaspoon pepper

1 teaspoon garlic powder

1⅓ cups french-fried onions

1 cup cheddar cheese, shredded

DIRECTIONS

1. Preheat the oven to 350°F. In a large bowl, stir together the green beans, mushroom soup, milk, salt, pepper, garlic powder, and ⅔ cup french-fried onions. Pour into a greased 1½-quart baking dish and bake for 15 minutes.

2. With an adult's help, add the cheddar cheese and the remaining ⅔ cup french-fried onions, and bake for another 5–10 minutes or until the cheese is melted.

Rapunzel's Pumpkin Hazelnut Stew

Serves 4 – 6

Hazelnut stew is Rapunzel's favorite dish any time of year, but there's nothing more perfect after a long day of wrapping gifts than this pumpkin version topped with crispy hazelnut bread crumbs.

Ingredients

For pumpkin stew:

1 tablespoon olive oil

1 shallot, diced

½ teaspoon salt

3 cups chicken or vegetable stock

1 cup unsweetened applesauce

¼ teaspoon pepper

⅛ teaspoon nutmeg

1 15-ounce can pumpkin puree

2 tablespoons brown sugar

½ cup sour cream

For hazelnut bread crumb topping:

½ tablespoon olive oil

¼ cup panko bread crumbs

¼ cup hazelnuts, chopped

Directions

To Make the Soup:

1. Have an adult help you warm the olive oil in a large pot over medium heat. Once the oil begins to simmer, add the shallot and salt. Cook, stirring occasionally, until the shallot becomes tender and translucent, about 7–8 minutes.

2. Add the chicken or vegetable stock, applesauce, pepper, nutmeg, pumpkin puree, and brown sugar, and simmer for 15 minutes. Add the sour cream and stir to combine.

To Make the Topping:

3. With an adult's help, heat the oil in a small pan over medium heat and add the bread crumbs. Stir them around until they're crisp and golden, about 3 minutes. Pour in the hazelnuts, and toast everything together for 2 minutes. Top each bowl of soup with a tablespoon of bread crumb topping.

DINNER

LIGHTNING MCQUEEN'S POT PIE

Serves 4

What's better than eating snowflakes on a cold winter's day? Eating a warm, flaky chicken pot pie!

INGREDIENTS

2 9-inch store-bought pie crusts, thawed

1 10½-ounce can condensed cream of chicken soup

½ cup milk

1 egg, lightly beaten

1 8-ounce package frozen mixed vegetables, thawed

1 cup chicken, cubed and cooked

1 teaspoon of salt

¼ teaspoon of pepper

¼ teaspoon of thyme

¼ teaspoon of nutmeg

DIRECTIONS

1. Heat oven to 375°F. Grease 4 small (4½- by 1¼-inch) aluminum pie tins or ovenproof bowls. Cut the two pie crusts into 8 individual pieces using the top of the pie tin as a guide. Line the bottom of each tin with 1 piece of crust. Using a small cookie cutter, cut out a small lightning bolt in the center of the remaining 4 pieces of crust.

2. In a medium bowl, whisk together the soup, milk, and egg. Mix in the vegetables, chicken, salt, pepper, thyme, and nutmeg.

3. Divide the filling among the 4 tins or bowls, cover each with a top crust, and crimp the edges together to seal. Have an adult help you trim any overhang.

4. With an adult's help, carefully place the pies in the oven, and bake until golden brown, 30–40 minutes. Let cool for 10 minutes before serving.

TIP: Leave out the chicken and substitute condensed cream of potato or mushroom soup for an equally delicious vegetable pie!

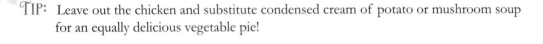

Olaf's Mini Pizzas

🍪🍪🍪 Makes 4

During the holidays, Olaf likes warm hugs and warm pizza! Take a break from the actual snow with these gooey snowman-shaped mini pizzas.

Ingredients

16 ounces of premade pizza dough

1 tablespoon olive oil or
cooking spray

1 cup pizza sauce

2 cups mozzarella cheese, shredded

Toppings:

Baby carrots, halved lengthwise

Capers

Sliced black olives

Pepperoni

Pretzel sticks

Directions

1. Allow pizza dough to sit at room temperature for at least 20 minutes. Separate the dough into 12 pieces and knead each piece into a ball.

2. Heat oven to 425°F. Cover a baking sheet with parchment paper, and grease paper with oil or cooking spray.

3. Working on a flour-dusted surface, roll the dough balls out until they are ¼-inch-thick circles.

4. Carefully transfer the circles to the baking sheet by first placing the bottom circle, then the center circle, overlapping the first slightly. Then add the head, overlapping the center circle slightly. Spread spoonfuls of pizza sauce on each of the 4 snowmen. Top the sauce with shredded mozzarella cheese.

5. Add the toppings to create Olaf's features: Use sliced black olives for his buttons and eyebrows, capers for his eyes, pretzel sticks for his arms and hair, and half a baby carrot for his nose. Have an adult help you cut a piece of pepperoni in half and then cut out a semicircle to create his silly grin.

6. Ask an adult to help you bake the pizzas in the oven until the edges and bottoms of the crusts are golden brown, about 6–8 minutes. Let the cooked pizzas cool slightly before serving.

WOODY'S COWBOY CHILI

 Serves 6

How does a true cowboy celebrate Christmas? With this simple chili that tastes even better the next day if it lasts that long!

INGREDIENTS

1 pound lean ground beef

1 cup onion, chopped

1 14½-ounce can stewed or roasted tomatoes

1 8-ounce can tomato sauce

1 15-ounce can dark red kidney beans, drained

1 15-ounce can light red kidney beans, drained

1 14-ounce can beef broth

2 teaspoons garlic powder

1 teaspoon salt

½ teaspoon pepper

1 cup cheddar cheese, shredded (optional)

DIRECTIONS

1. Place the beef and onion in a large pot and have an adult help you cook them over medium-high heat until the meat is brown and the onions are tender.

2. Add the remaining ingredients except for the cheddar cheese to the pot. Stir, bring to a boil, and reduce heat to low.

3. Cover partially and let simmer for 30–45 minutes (the longer it simmers, the thicker your chili will be). Serve with a sprinkling of shredded cheddar cheese if you like.

MERIDA'S FAMOUS DAY-AFTER-CHRISTMAS SLIDERS

 Makes 12

Merida's triplet brothers can be picky, but they all can agree that her sliders are their favorite! They love anything that comes in sets of three, and these small turkey sliders can be customized with any combination of three toppings: cranberry sauce, stuffing, and gravy.

INGREDIENTS

For sliders:

1 pound lean ground turkey

¼ cup bread crumbs

2 teaspoons onion powder

1 clove garlic, crushed

1 teaspoon kosher salt

½ teaspoon ground pepper

12 whole-wheat slider rolls

For toppings:

1 package stuffing

1 12-ounce can cranberry sauce

1 jar turkey or chicken gravy

DIRECTIONS

1. Prepare the stuffing according to the package instructions.

2. In a medium-sized bowl, combine the ground turkey, bread crumbs, onion powder, garlic, salt, and pepper. Form eight 3-inch-wide patties.

3. Spray a large pan with cooking spray, and with the help of an adult, heat it over medium heat. Add the patties, and cook until browned, about 5 minutes per side. Remove from the pan.

4. Warm the gravy in the microwave. Spread cranberry sauce on one side of the buns. Place the patties on the buns, mound a small amount of stuffing on each, and top with the gravy.

Serves 4

Lady and Tramp celebrate Christmas by recreating their first pasta date! Zucchini ribbons topped with mini chicken meatballs are a festive alternative to their signature dish.

INGREDIENTS

For meatballs:

1 pound ground chicken or turkey

2 cloves garlic, crushed

1 teaspoon onion powder

1 teaspoon dried basil

½ teaspoon salt

½ teaspoon pepper

¼ cup bread crumbs

1 teaspoon olive oil

1 24-ounce jar pasta sauce

For zucchini pasta:

4 zucchinis, with or without skin

1 teaspoon olive oil

1 teaspoon garlic powder

1 teaspoon salt

½ teaspoon pepper

Parmesan cheese (optional)

DIRECTIONS

TO MAKE THE MEATBALLS:

1. Combine the ground chicken or turkey, garlic, onion powder, basil, salt, pepper, and bread crumbs in a large bowl and mix until combined. Roll into small balls and set aside.

2. Have an adult help you heat the olive oil in a large skillet over medium heat. Add the meatballs and brown for 1 minute. Pour in jar of pasta sauce and stir gently to mix. Put on the lid, turn the heat down to low, and allow the meatballs to simmer for 20 minutes.

TO MAKE THE ZUCCHINI PASTA:

3. Have an adult help you cut the ends off each zucchini. Using a box grater placed on its side with the largest holes facing up, carefully grate each zucchini lengthwise in long strokes. Make sure to ask for help grating once you've reached the end of the zucchini.

4. Heat the olive oil in a skillet over medium-high heat. Add the zucchini, sprinkle with the garlic powder, salt, and pepper, and cook for 2–3 minutes or until the "noodles" are cooked through yet firm.

5. Divide the zucchini into 4 bowls, and ladle on a few meatballs and sauce. Top with Parmesan cheese, if desired.

To Infinity and Beyond Meat Loaf

 Serves 6

Buzz Lightyear takes pride in building his snow Space Rangers. But what every Space Ranger needs is a rocket ship to travel to the moon and back!

Ingredients

For the loaves:

¼ cup ketchup

½ small onion, minced

1 teaspoon olive oil

1 pound ground turkey or beef

½ cup bread crumbs

1 egg

½ teaspoon oregano

½ teaspoon basil

1 teaspoon salt

¼ teaspoon pepper

½ of a small zucchini, grated (optional)

½ of a carrot, peeled and grated (optional)

For the sauce:

¼ cup ketchup

4 teaspoons Worcestershire sauce

Directions

To Make the Sauce:

1. Mix together the ketchup and Worcestershire sauce in a small bowl and set aside.

To Make the Meat Loaf:

2. Preheat the oven to 350°F. Line a 9- by 13-inch baking pan with aluminum foil, then spray with cooking spray and set aside.

3. Combine all of the meat loaf ingredients in a large bowl with your hands. Scoop out a handful of the meat mixture, and form it into a rocket shape on the baking sheet, adding more of the mixture for each wing.

4. Have an adult help you place the pan in the oven, and then bake for 40–50 minutes. Carefully remove the sheet and let it sit for 5 minutes before moving the meat loaves to a plate. Decorate each loaf with the sauce and serve.

SIDES & DRINKS

WRECK-IT RALPH'S SMASHED POTATOES

 Serves 4

Have fun smashing these roasted potatoes just like Ralph to make a great, easy side for any holiday meal.

INGREDIENTS

1–2 teaspoons kosher salt

Ground pepper, to taste

½ cup extra virgin olive oil

12 small potatoes (such as red bliss)

DIRECTIONS

1. Fill a large pot with water, add about 1 teaspoon of salt, and then add the potatoes. Have an adult help you set it over high heat until the water begins to boil, and then turn the heat down to medium-low and let it simmer for about 20 minutes, or until the potatoes feel soft when you insert a fork.

2. Preheat the oven to 450°F. While the potatoes cook, line a baking pan with aluminum foil and coat it with cooking spray. Once an adult has carefully removed the potatoes from the water, arrange them on the pan so that they are evenly spaced.

3. Using the bottom of a glass, press down on each potato to smash it. Once all the potatoes are smashed, drizzle them with olive oil and season with salt and pepper.

4. Have an adult help you place the baking pan on the top rack of the oven, and roast the potatoes for 20–25 minutes or until crispy and brown at the edges. Remove from the oven and let them cool down before you enjoy them!

TIP: If you're short on time, you can boil and smash these potatoes the night before and store them in the refrigerator. The next day, just let the potatoes come to room temperature before placing them in the oven.

ALADDIN'S CINNAMON APPLES

🍪🍪🍪 Serves 4 – 6

Aladdin is always inspired by his trips to the marketplace, no matter what season it is! His signature holiday dinner side is safely cut with an apple slicer and easily simmered in 15 minutes.

INGREDIENTS

4 medium apples, peeled (McIntosh or Granny Smith work best)

½ cup light brown sugar

1 teaspoon ground cinnamon

¼ teaspoon ground nutmeg

4 tablespoons water

1 tablespoon butter

DIRECTIONS

1. Slice apples with an apple slicer. In a medium bowl, toss together apples, light brown sugar, cinnamon, and nutmeg.

2. Put apple mixture, water, and butter into a medium-sized saucepan, and have an adult help you cook it over medium heat, stirring occasionally, until apples are tender, 14–16 minutes.

TIP: If the glaze becomes too thick, thin it by adding a tablespoon of water at a time until it is the right consistency.

Never Land Hot Chocolate with Star Marshmallows

Serves 4

How do you get to Never Land? Why, fly to the second star to the right and straight on till morning. Even Santa follows these directions to deliver Christmas presents to the Lost Boys!

INGREDIENTS

For marshmallows:

2 tablespoons (2 packets) gelatin

2 cups granulated sugar

¼ teaspoon salt

2 teaspoons vanilla extract

2 tablespoons silver sprinkles

¾ cup confectioners' sugar

For cocoa:

1 quart whole milk

⅓ cup unsweetened cocoa powder

½ cup sugar

3 crushed peppermint sticks

Pinch of salt

For gift jar:

2¼ cups unsweetened cocoa powder

12 crushed peppermint sticks

3½ cups sugar

1 tablespoon salt

DIRECTIONS

TO MAKE THE MARSHMALLOWS:

1. Add ½ cup cold water to a small bowl and sprinkle the gelatin mixture on top. Set it aside for 10 minutes. Line a 9- by 13-inch baking pan with cling wrap, then spray it liberally with cooking spray. Set aside the pan for now.

2. With an adult's help, place the granulated sugar and ½ cup cold water into a large saucepan and stir over medium heat until dissolved. Add the gelatin and bring to a boil. Remove from the heat and carefully pour the mixture into a large bowl and let stand until partially cool.

3. Add the salt and vanilla extract, and beat with an electric mixer until it is soft and doubles in volume, about 10–15 minutes. Pour the mixture into the pan and smooth it into the corners with a spatula sprayed with cooking oil. Set it aside until it becomes firm, about 3 hours.

4. Flip the marshmallows over and remove the cling wrap. Dust the sprinkles on top and cut out with a small star-shaped cookie cutter sprayed with cooking spray. Dip the bottom and edges of each star in confectioners' sugar, and set aside.

TO MAKE THE COCOA:

5. Have an adult help you heat the milk in a large saucepan over medium-low heat. Be careful not to let it boil. Add the remaining ingredients, stir to dissolve, and pour into four individual mugs. Top with 1 or 2 marshmallows.

ASSEMBLING A GIFT JAR:

 In a large bowl, whisk together the cocoa powder, sugar, and salt. Pour the mixture into a pint-sized (16-ounce) mason jar and top with peppermint sticks and marshmallows. Close the jar tightly, and attach the recipe card from the back of the book.

ARIEL'S STARFISH DIP

🍪 Serves 6

There's nothing that gets you into the holiday spirit more than Christmas shopping! These sea-inspired mouthfuls are quick to whip up and are especially yummy after a busy day looking for the perfect gifts to put under the tree!

INGREDIENTS

1 10-ounce package frozen spinach, thawed

½ cup low-fat mayonnaise

1 package onion soup mix

1 8-ounce container low-fat sour cream

2 cucumbers, sliced into 1-inch rounds

½ red pepper, cut into 1-inch-thick strips and then sliced on the diagonal

½ green pepper, cut into 1-inch-thick strips and then sliced on the diagonal

DIRECTIONS

1. Squeeze the spinach to remove any excess water. Put the spinach, mayonnaise, onion soup mix, and sour cream into a large bowl and combine.

2. Using the back of a small spoon, smear about a teaspoon of dip onto one side of a cucumber round. Arrange 5 pieces of pepper to give the appearance of a starfish, and serve.

STITCH'S HAWAIIAN EGGNOG

 Serves 4

Lilo and Stitch like to make eggnog but with a special Hawaiian twist!

INGREDIENTS

1½ cups whole milk

½ cup heavy cream

½ cup cream of coconut

4 large eggs

1 16-ounce can pineapple juice

¼ cup brown sugar

2 teaspoons vanilla extract

½ teaspoon ground cinnamon

¼ teaspoon nutmeg

⅛ teaspoon ground cloves

4 pineapple wedges (optional)

DIRECTIONS

1. Add the milk, cream, cream of coconut, eggs, pineapple juice, and brown sugar to a large pot and whisk to combine.

2. Have an adult help you heat the mixture over low heat, whisking constantly, until it thickens slightly (about 10–15 minutes). Do not let it boil.

3. Remove the pot from the heat and stir in the vanilla extract and spices. Garnish with a pineapple wedge, if desired, and serve immediately.

JASMINE'S YUMMY YOGURT DIP

Serves 2–3

For Jasmine, this dish really hits the spot after she wins a snowball fight against Aladdin! She enjoys celebrating with some yummy carrots and her favorite yogurt dip.

INGREDIENTS

Carrots

1 5.3-ounce container of plain Greek yogurt

½ tablespoon (about a quarter) freshly squeezed lemon juice

½ teaspoon dried oregano

¼ teaspoon salt

Pinch of ground pepper

DIRECTIONS

1. Combine the container of yogurt, lemon juice, oregano, salt, and pepper in a small bowl and mix with a spoon. Serve alongside the carrots.

DESSERT

SUGAR RUSH POPCORN GUMDROP GARLAND

Makes 1 36-inch garland

Vanellope loves decorating her tree with this seasonal garland. With Ralph's help, reaching the top branches is no trouble at all! Plus, this holiday treat is just as good to nibble on!

INGREDIENTS

1 package of popcorn, popped and cooled

2 16-ounce bags of multicolored gumdrops

Tray of Never Land Star Marshmallows, page 44 or regular marshmallows

DIRECTIONS

1. Have an adult help you thread a blunt sewing needle with a fishing line, thread, or even unflavored waxed dental floss. Leave the tail end attached to the spool.

2. Choose a pattern of popcorn, marshmallows, and gumdrops to repeat. Begin stringing the pieces by piercing the needle through the center of each object and pushing the object down along the string.

3. Once your garland is long enough, have an adult help you cut the thread from the spool and tie knots at both ends to secure.

TIP: Make sure to use cooled, or even day-old, popcorn—it's easier to string!

Jiminy Cricket Milkshake

 Serves 2

This milkshake is a peppermint-and-chocolate delight, fit for a "real boy" (or girl)!

INGREDIENTS

For the whipped cream:

½ cup heavy cream

½ teaspoon vanilla extract

½ tablespoon confectioners' sugar

For the milkshake:

4–6 scoops of your favorite mint chocolate chip ice cream

¼ cup whole milk

6 chocolate sandwich cookies

DIRECTIONS

1. Leave the ice cream out on the counter for about 10 minutes to soften.

TO MAKE THE WHIPPED CREAM:

2. Add the heavy cream to a medium bowl. With a handheld whisk or electric mixer with a whisk attachment, whip the cream until it begins to thicken (when you lift the whisk from the bowl, the cream should stick slightly to the whisk and fall over).

3. Add the vanilla extract and sugar to the bowl, and continue whisking until the cream's peaks can stand up on their own. Be careful not to overwhisk!

TO MAKE THE MILKSHAKE:

4. Blend the ice cream, milk, and 4 cookies in a blender until combined. Pour into two glasses and top with whipped cream, and 2 crumbled cookies like in the photo.

ANNA'S FROZEN ICE CANDY

 Makes 2

Anna loves the icicles her sister, Elsa, makes so much that she wants to make her own! These ice candy crystals are a tasty spin on Elsa's amazing creations.

INGREDIENTS

½ cup water

2 ¾ cups sugar

Blue food coloring

DIRECTIONS

1. With an adult's help, heat the water in a saucepan over medium-high heat until it comes to a boil. Add the sugar ¼ cup at a time, and stir continuously with a wooden spoon until the sugar dissolves completely (try not to let it boil). Add 8–10 drops of blue food coloring, stir until combined, and carefully remove the saucepan from the heat.

2. Attach a clothespin to the tops of two wooden skewers. Using the clothespin as a handle, dip each skewer into the sugar solution, and roll them in plain sugar. Put them aside to dry while allowing the sugar solution to cool for about 5 minutes.

3. Divide the solution to fill two large water glasses or jars about ¾ full. Slowly insert one skewer into each glass so that it rests about 2–3 inches from the bottom and sides of the glass. Set your glasses up in a warm location where they will not be disturbed.

4. Crystals will begin to form in an hour, and continue growing for a few days. After about a week, they will be large enough to eat!

POOH BEAR'S MINI HONEY BUNS

 Makes 8 – 10

Pooh Bear loves opening presents almost as much as he loves honey! This well-loved Christmas dessert is quick to make and delicious enough to share.

INGREDIENTS

2 tablespoons brown sugar

1 teaspoon cinnamon

$^1/_3$ cup unsalted butter

$^1/_3$ cup honey

1 tube refrigerated biscuits

DIRECTIONS

1. Preheat oven to 350°F. Combine the brown sugar and cinnamon in a small bowl and set aside.

2. Place the butter in another small bowl and melt it in the microwave. Stir in the honey. Divide half of the mixture evenly among 8–10 cups of a standard-sized muffin tin.

3. Separate the biscuits and roll each one into a rope. Coil each rope into a circle and pinch each end of the rope into the coil next to it so it is secure (or else they will unravel). Place each honey bun into a muffin tin cup, top with the remaining honey mixture, and sprinkle evenly with the brown sugar topping.

4. Bake for 12–15 minutes. Allow them to cool completely before serving.

SHERWOOD FOREST PEPPERMINT BARK

 Serves 6

This classic Christmas dessert is knotted with crushed peppermint and marshmallows, which always reminds Robin Hood of the old knotted trees in his beloved Sherwood Forest. He loves to give this out during the holidays because it is like sharing pieces of home with his friends!

Ingredients

1 pound white chocolate, chips or a chopped bar

½ cup candy canes or starlight mints, crushed

½ cup mini marshmallows

Directions

1. Line a 9- by 13-inch baking pan with parchment paper or aluminum foil. Set aside.

2. Place the white chocolate in a bowl and microwave for 30 seconds. Have an adult help you remove the bowl in case it is hot, stir the chocolate with a spatula, and place it back in the microwave. Continue to microwave the chocolate in 30-second periods until it has all melted.

3. Pour the chocolate into the baking pan and smooth it out with the spatula. Quickly sprinkle on the candy cane pieces and marshmallows, and lightly press them into the chocolate. Let the bark harden for at least an hour at room temperature before breaking into pieces.

TIP: It's easy to crush candy canes, even without a blender. Just add a few candy canes to a zip-top bag and crush them with a rolling pin.

Assembling a Gift Jar:

 Layer the ingredients from above in a pint-sized (16-ounce) mason jar in the following order: chocolate chips, candy cane or starlight mints, and mini marshmallows. Close the jar tightly and attach the recipe card from the back of the book.

SIMBA'S MUDDY BROWNIES

Makes 12

Simba loves to dig around in the mud for grubs to eat with Timon and Pumbaa, and you'll have fun eating these gooey mud brownies topped with red and green gummy worms!

INGREDIENTS

For the brownies:

1 cup all-purpose flour

½ cup unsweetened cocoa powder

¼ teaspoon salt

½ cup (1 stick) unsalted butter

1 cup sugar

2 eggs

1 teaspoon vanilla extract

For the mud frosting:

½ cup (1 stick) unsalted butter

⅓ cup unsweetened cocoa powder

1½ cups confectioners' sugar

1 teaspoon vanilla extract

⅓ cup milk

2 4-ounce bags gummy worms

DIRECTIONS

TO MAKE THE BROWNIES:

1. Preheat the oven to 350°F. Grease a 9- by 13-inch baking dish and set aside.

2. Whisk together the flour, cocoa powder, and salt in a small bowl and set aside. Using an electric mixer, cream the butter and sugar until light and fluffy, about 3 minutes. Add the eggs and vanilla until combined, and then gradually add the dry ingredients.

3. Pour the mix into the baking dish. With an adult's help, place it into the oven and bake for about 25 minutes or until a toothpick inserted into the center comes out clean.

TO MAKE THE MUD FROSTING:

4. With an adult's help, melt the butter and cocoa together in a medium saucepan over medium heat. Mix in the confectioners' sugar and vanilla until smooth, and gradually add the milk while continuing to stir until the frosting has reached a nice muddy consistency. Let the frosting stand for a minute or two, then spread it over the brownies and top with the gummy worms.

ASSEMBLING A GIFT JAR:

Layer the following ingredients from above in a pint-sized (16-ounce) mason jar in this order: flour, salt, cocoa powder, sugar, and gummy worms. Close the jar tightly and attach the recipe card from the back of the book.

Food styling by Jenny Park

Designed by Tony Fejeran and Margaret Peng

Special thanks to Elizabeth Schaefer, Tomas Palacios, Eric Geron, Brittany Candau, and Mike Siglain

Printed in the United States of America

First Edition
10 9 8 7 6 5 4 3 2 1
G942-9090-6-14213
Library of Congress Control Number: 2014934614
ISBN 978-1-4231-6322-0

For more Disney Press fun, visit www.disneybooks.com